THE NASTY✿WOMAN RESISTANCE

LOOK FOR OTHER MARIE RIVERS COLORING BOOKS:

UPLIFTING MESSAGES OF HOPE FOR UNCERTAIN TIMES

#WETHEPEOPLE COLORING BOOK

FOLLOW MARIE RIVERS ON FACEBOOK!
WWW.FACEBOOK.COM/MARIERIVERSCOLORING

AND FIND MARIE RIVERS T-SHIRTS AT:
WWW.MARIERIVERS.THREADLESS.COM

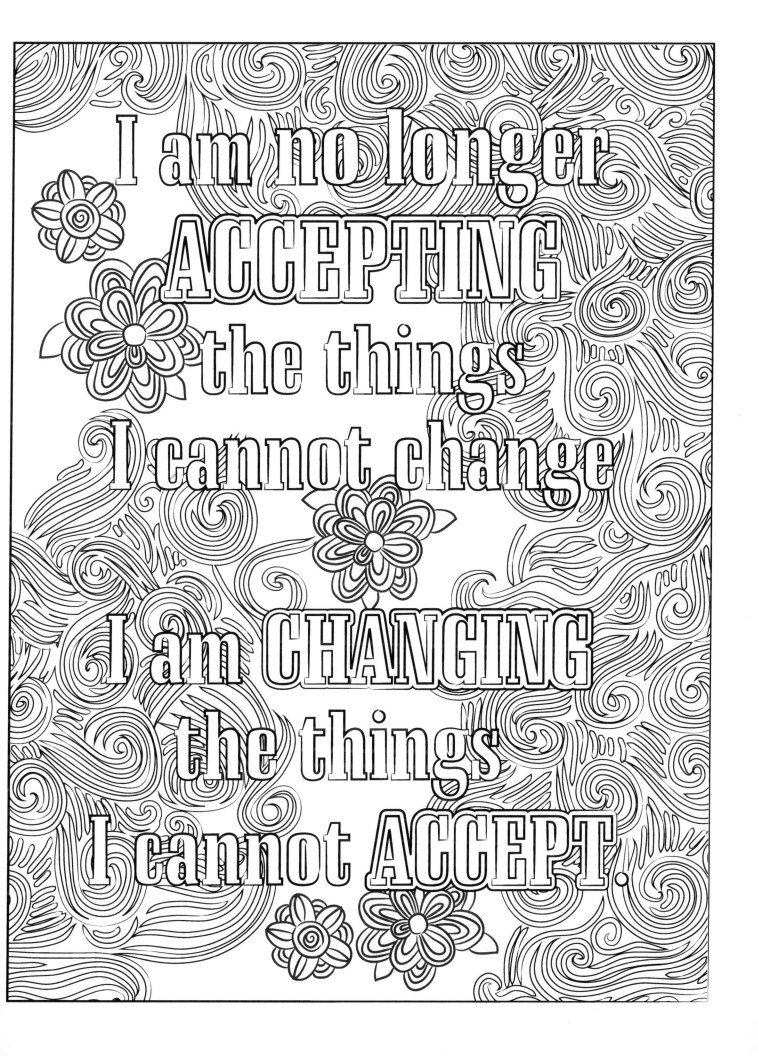

nas·ty wom·an

/'nastē'wōōmən/

noun

a confident, independent female

O'Connor&
Ginsburg&
Sotomayor&
Kagan.

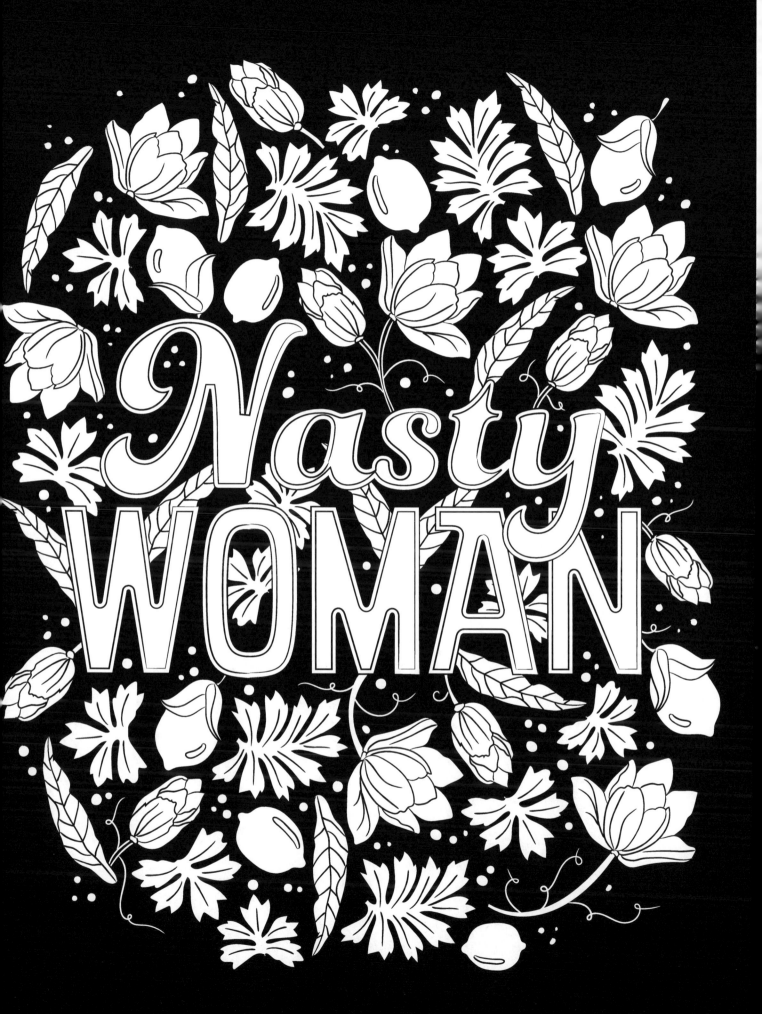

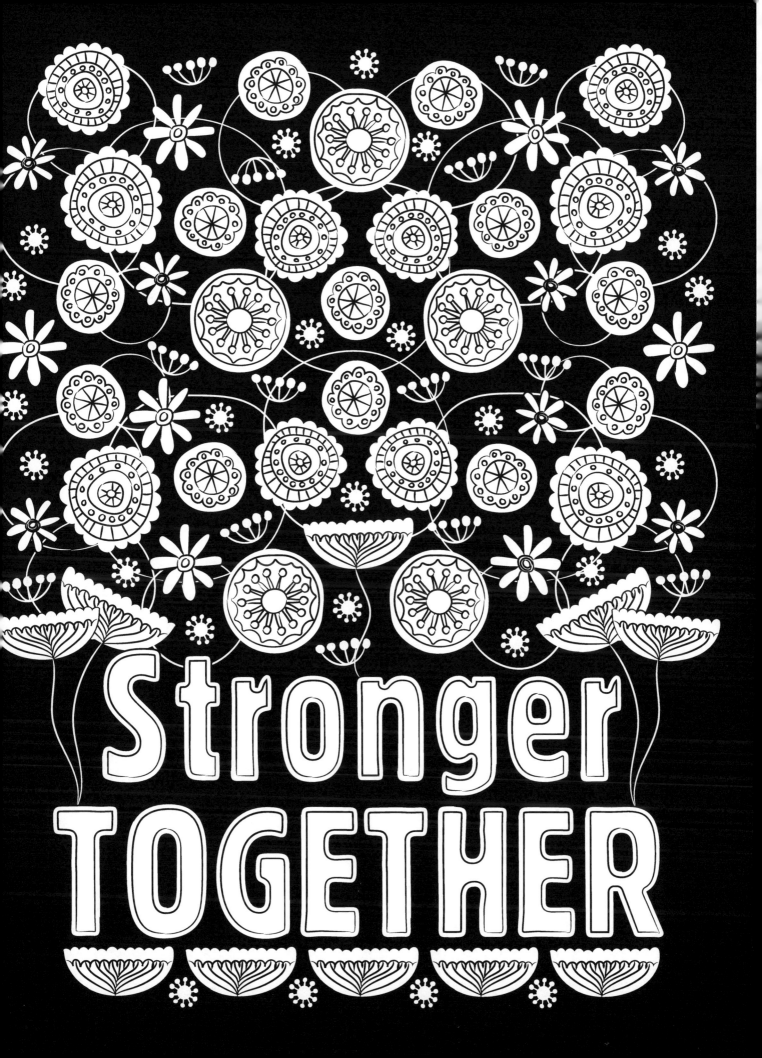

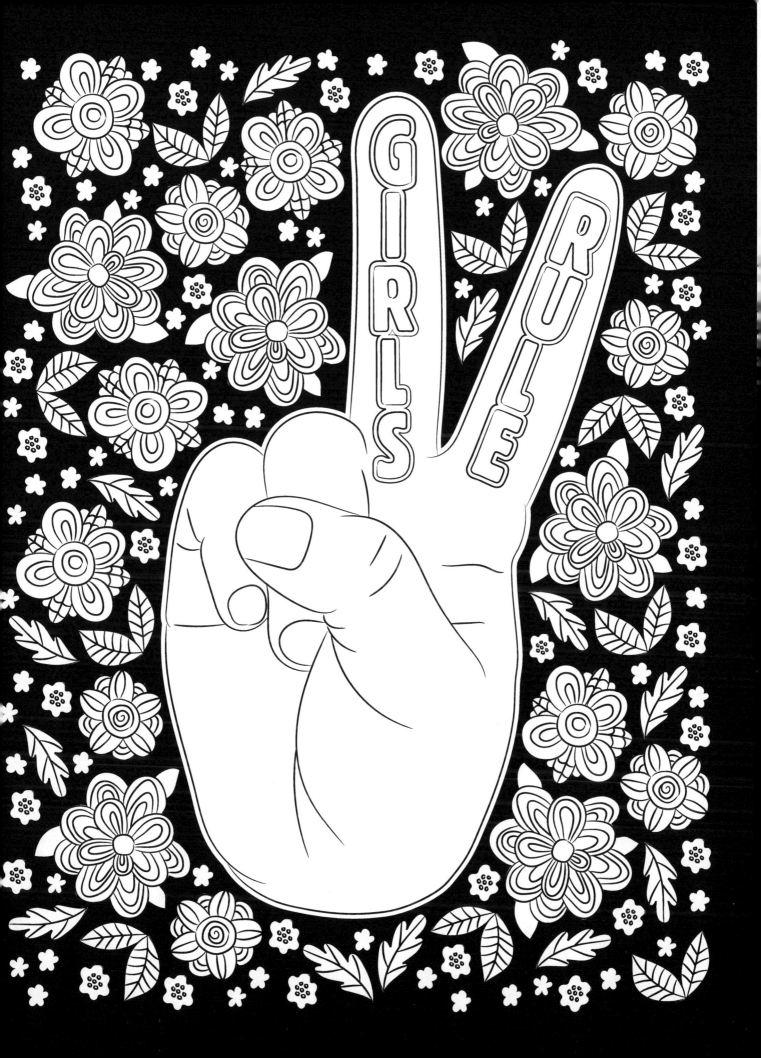

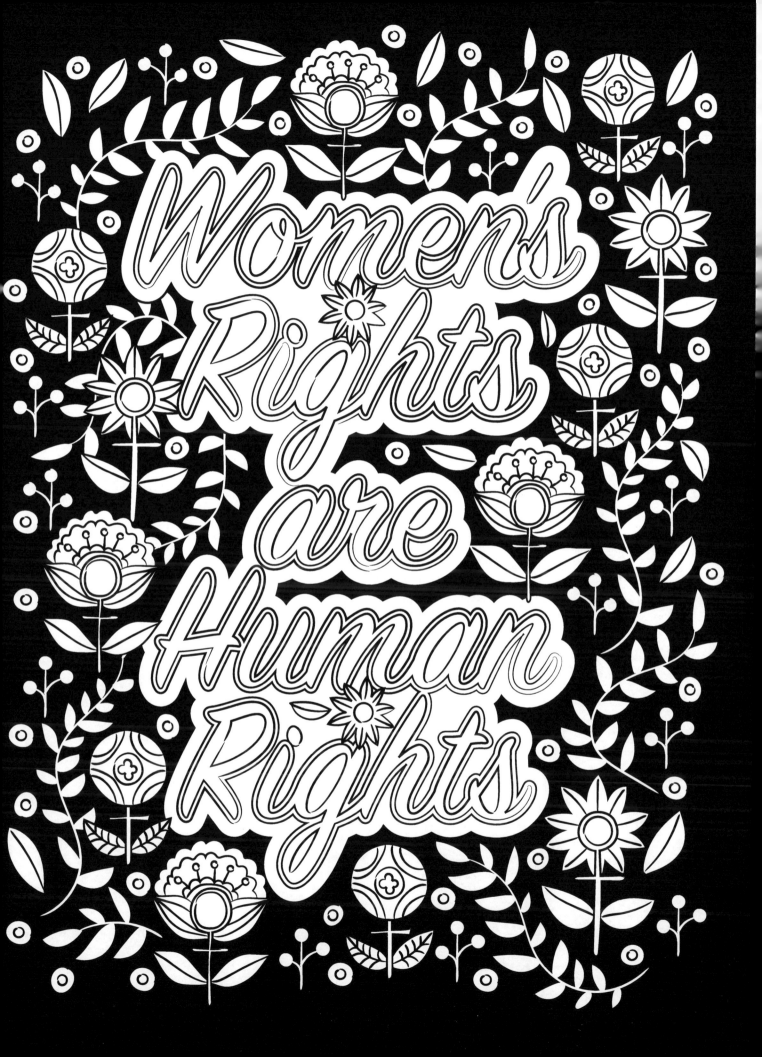

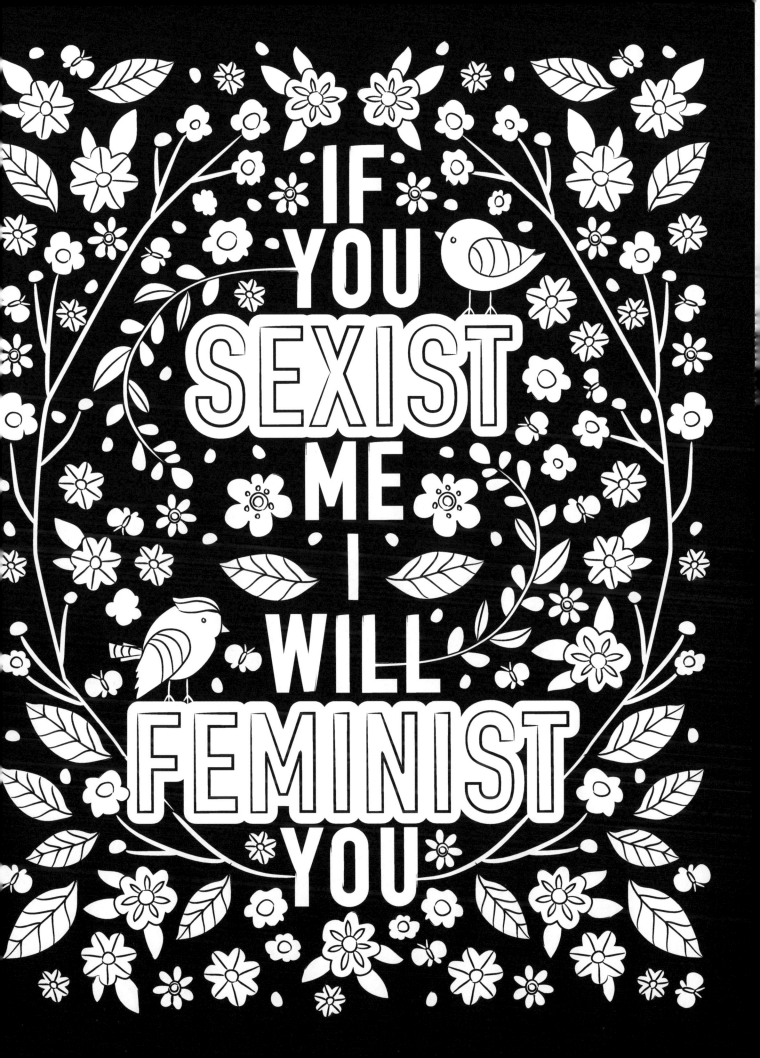

nas·ty wom·an

/ˈnaste ˈwo͞oměn/
noun
a confident, independent female

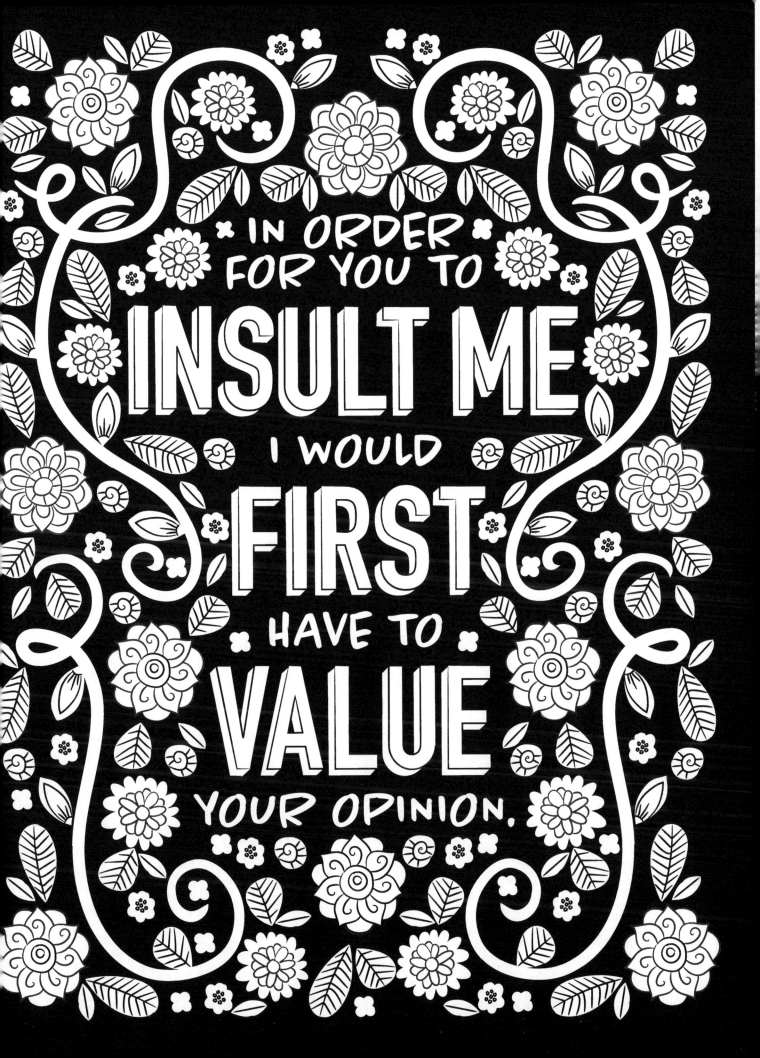

Here's to
STRONG WOMEN.
May we
KNOW THEM.
May we
BE THEM.
May we
RAISE THEM.

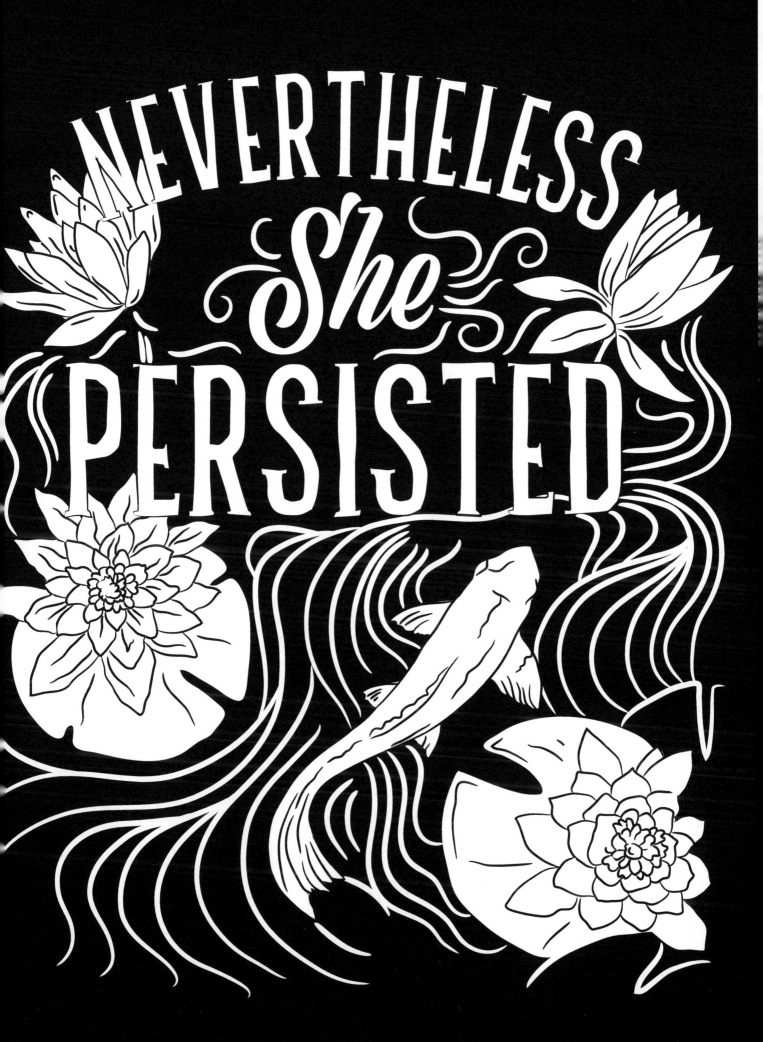

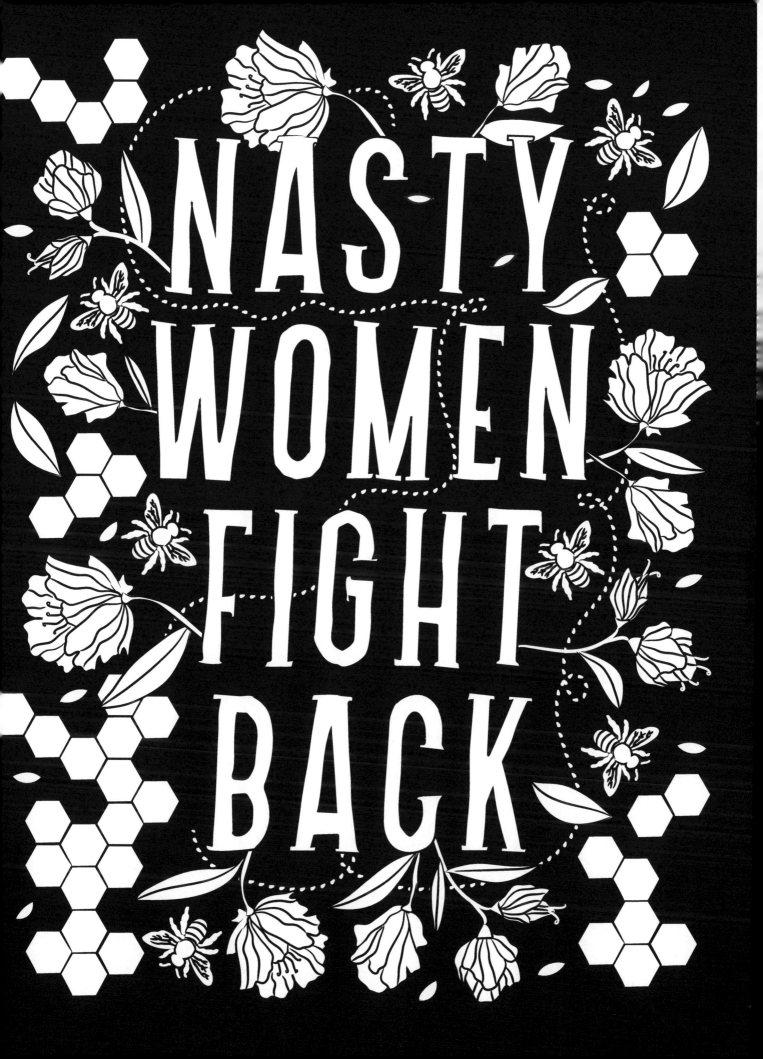

O'Connor&
Ginsburg&
Sotomayor&
Kagan.

Made in the USA
Middletown, DE
02 January 2018